P A T R I C I A   J A F F E

Women Engravers

V I R A G O

Published by VIRAGO PRESS Limited 1990
20–23 Mandela Street, Camden Town, London NW1 0HQ

First published in Great Britain by VIRAGO PRESS 1988

ISBN 0 86068 188 2

A CIP catalogue record for this book is available from The British Library.

Typeset in Linotron Meridien by
Goodfellow & Egan (Phototypesetting) Ltd

Printed in Great Britain by
St Edmundsbury Press, Bury St Edmunds, Suffolk

This book has been conceived, produced and designed by
SILENT BOOKS, Swavesey, Cambridge CB4 5RA

The engravings on the title page and chapter openings
have been specially commissioned from Deborah Jaffé,
Student (Printmaking), Central School of
Arts and Crafts 1986–89.

FOREWORD

Women this century have adopted wood-engraving. With so many using it as a medium natural to them, an essay such as mine cannot hope to do justice to everyone. Some have had brief fame, some sustained: others have never had the recognition their artistic talents deserve. What is important is that women have found another means of expression. This volume gives an opportunity to illustrate a variety of their prints, but within limits of size, space and black and white reproduction. To the many fine contemporary women wood-engravers whose work is omitted, my apologies: I have focused on the pioneers. I dedicate the work to my mother – not an engraver, but of that generation which has lived through two wars and seen the ways of women change.

OOD-ENGRAVING is an intense exercise, usually solitary, and often minute. The block itself is beautiful, at its best a piece of boxwood. It is always highly polished, often comfortably small, with all the appeal of a perfectly formed, miniature object. Its usual colour is some shade of honey from the brightest gold or amber, to the more shadowy, sombre tones from a wild bees' nest. It sits invitingly ready to spin slowly on an old leather-bound book or an engraver's sand-bag, which is curved, polished and circular, two leather saucers stitched face to face, filled, heavy, solid. The tools, since every engraver has his or her own adapted to their individual engraving hand, work as an extension to one's fingers. A semicircular boxwood handle will press against the heel of the palm and the steel shaft, curving slightly upwards from that plane established by the flattened face of the handle, will protrude about half an inch beyond the comfortably curved index finger. A sense of excitement in contemplating the pristine block must be, to some degree, a common experience for all engravers. A new block is like that tiny door for Alice in Wonderland: the engraver bends down and peers through into a scene which it seems almost impossible to achieve. The tools will pick and stroke little pieces out of the surface of that wood, the engraver enjoying – as a potter does – the intimacy of two hands working together on one design; the free hand is busy turning the block upon the polished leather, moving it onto the point of the tool if a long curve is wanted, or positioning it for a cut at a different angle. What are removed are those parts which will appear white in the finished print; the progression is from darkness towards light. Once one has begun, the sensation of something becoming brighter between one's hands is very real and absorbing. That beginning is often preceded by a slight hiatus: terror. But like all moments of pause before action, it is exhilarating.

The reward is a print which could have been achieved in no other way, and one which, when sensitively reproduced by a skilled craftsman, may be multiplied thousands of times. The satisfaction of seeing those myriads

Decorated capital letter engraved by Mary Byfield (1795–1871) for Charles Whittingham at the Chiswick Press, and used in Oliver Byrne's *The First Six Books of the Elements of Euclid*, 1847.

of identical impressions after such a long gestation period is immense. The combination of patience, intensity and long-term planning, as well as the domestic scale of most engraving, strikes an immediate chord in female understanding. Yet until this century wood-engraving has remained a male-dominated craft. It would be fascinating to discover why this should have happened, and what has brought about the sensational flowering of talent among women engravers in the twentieth century. But one can never explain any artistic achievement fully: why do mushroom spores lie dormant for many seasons and then one autumn flush white across the fields? One can only guess and surmise. 'Of all media,' said Clare Leighton, 'wood-engraving is the one in which there is the least to be taught and the most to be learnt.' And learning is an individual, private matter. So here goes for my wild surmise.

Despite the Frenchman Papillon's gallant but fantastical attempt to promote the Italian Isabella Cunio equally with her twin brother as the attractively aristocratic thirteenth-century initiator of the genre, wood-engraving has remained an art chiefly led by the English-speaking nations, and women played a relatively small part in any branch of its development. However, since 1900 Britain has made up for lost time, producing a significant number of women wood-engravers. At least six of them, Joan Hassall, Gertrude Hermes, Clare Leighton, Agnes Miller Parker, Monica Poole and Gwen Raverat, have engraved outstanding work which can take its place in any account of the medium, and today there are several equally promising engravers among younger women artists. It does seem a strange phenomenon, this flourishing band of women print-makers, but on closer examination one sees that the mystery is not that they have appeared now, but that their equals should have been denied the chance to appear a century earlier. The reasons probably lie not in the craft itself, but in economics, the apprenticeship system and the status of women. Moreover the term 'wood-engraver' has changed its meaning more than once during the last two hundred years, and that change of emphasis is not irrelevant to our inquiry.

Use the term 'wood-engraver' of a contemporary in the late twentieth century, and you are bound to be referring to an artist-craftsman, male or female. Use the term of someone working one hundred years ago and as like as not you refer to a technician trained during the course of a thoroughgoing apprenticeship and esteemed and rewarded according to the degree of skill he had attained: that wood-engraver is sure to be male. Use the term of someone working two hundred years ago and, almost inevitably, you are talking of Thomas Bewick who took the metal engraver's tools from his apprenticeship days and moved them over, from gun barrels and the like, to work on the end grain of boxwood. The resulting blocks, superb and subtle themselves, could actually be locked up in a chase along with type and printed in one fell swoop – inking and impression – an economic innovation whose commercial application was rapidly seized upon. Despite Bewick's comparative isolation in remote Northumberland England, end grain boxwood engraving spread world-wide. Thomas Bewick was an artist-engraver: he and the apprentices in his workshop made drawings and water-colours of the subjects they wished to depict and they then worked an interprative engraving upon wood, reversing the image where necessary. In the history of wood-engraving the names of these apprentices are familiar, but as commerce elevated them, the pressures of commerce also undermined the art which Bewick had taught them.

Some, like Luke Clennell, were skilled at cutting away the wood to leave lines standing in relief, so fine and with such a subtle swell that one could almost swear that they were drawn into the book with pen and ink: this has come to be known as black line engraving, and is often frowned upon. Artistically the skill was Clennell's undoing: he was commissioned by publishers not as an artist-craftsman but to reproduce work by established illustrators: you can find Luke Clennell's superb engravings in Samuel Roger's *Pleasures of Memory*, but the original drawings for the designs were made by Thomas Stothard. Clennell is credited there as the engraver, but he is little known today as artist or designer. Publishers wanted only the skill and speed of the young man's craft, and into this trap most nineteenth-century master wood-engravers were to fall. Another of Bewick's apprentices, William Harvey, demonstrates the other route down the slippery slope away from the self rule of artist-craftsman wood-engraver: he drew and engraved beautifully, making delicious little blocks of rural scenes, richer and more thickly wooded than Bewick's because they depicted the agriculturally more hospitable and prosperous south. Once in a while he engraved after other artists, but his own designs were much in demand and when his reputation was well established the inevitable happened; he began to farm the engravings out. You can see the commercial pressure that snared him: one draws much faster than one can engrave and, since fewer people can draw well than can learn to control a burin, it made economic sense for one man to make many designs and many engravers to work on them simultaneously. In this way the intimate relationship between design and engraving, established by Thomas Bewick, was almost completely lost in the course of the next generation, and the division beween artist and reproductive engraver became accepted as natural.

There were only a very few independent artists who, inspired by Bewick's achievements, but apparently self-taught, experimented with wood-engraving. Chief among them were William Blake, Edward Calvert and Samuel Palmer, and for each, wood-engraving was the least of his artistic endeavours: their experiments were to have little influence until the turn of this century.

Meanwhile, as literacy spread, thanks to the Victorians' determined drive for universal education, the demand for literature increased. Wood-engraving combined so perfectly and inexpensively with type that it had become the commonest means of illustrating printed works. Firms were established which dealt solely in making reproductive wood-engravings. These were universally regarded as necessary commercial enterprises providing the cheapest and most expeditious means by which illustrations could be printed. The finest work was now at a premium, and the skilful engraver was a master of a valued and lucrative craft whose methods and techniques were, in the way of trade associations, guarded. The apprentice-ship system was still the usual means by which a tradesman learned his craft, the apprentices living with the master as part of his household, often lodging in a sort of boys' dormitory which by its nature excluded the propriety or even the possibility of taking on female pupils. There were also deeper reasons for the craft of wood-engraving being inaccessible to women. This was a profession, and women did not become professionals. Not one of Thomas Bewick's three daughters is known as a wood-engraver, although his eldest, Jane, was his closest confidante and the very individual for whom he wrote his account of his life and experience as an engraver. Only Bewick's son, Robert, was apprenticed to his father. Ladies busied themselves with homely amusements. Half a century later, in 1856, when Ward and Lock published their *Elegant Arts for Ladies* the arts described, Feather Flowers, Rice Shell Work, Painting on Velvet, Porcupine Quill Work, Calisthenic Exercises, Waxen Flowers and Fruit, etc., are illustrated with wood-engravings, but the technique is not included in 'the whole range of what we have deemed proper to style Elegant Arts for Ladies'. This seems the more surprising as, from the 1860s onwards, printing itself was advertised as an appropriate feminine hobby. Mrs Daniel Jones exhibited her miniature Albion at the 1862 Exhibition and 'undertook to instruct ladies in the mysteries of printing'. But professionals resented amateurs as intruders, and suppliers refused to deal with anyone who was not in the trade. The engravings in *Elegant Arts for Ladies* were made by the most celebrated Victorian firm, the Brothers Dalziel, and it may well have been that, through the guarded professionalism of such firms, suppliers were prevailed upon to withhold both tools and materials from amateurs.

Nor is wood-engraving covered in 'a sociological study' edited by J. Ramsay Macdonald, which surveys the 60 years from 1841 to 1901, and was published in London in 1904, *Women in the Printing Trade*. This makes it clear that women were taken on as hired hands in their young unmarried years: most left work when they married. A pitiful few returned if they were widowed. To give young girls any skill training must have seemed a bad investment to employers: female employees in the printing trades progressed little further than learning to make envelopes.

It was not until a day-school system was established for arts and crafts that women could find the opportunity to learn skills which, under the apprenticeship system, had been the province of men. The Schools of Design in Britain began with the establishment, by Lord Melbourne's government, of the Normal School of Design. It opened on 1 June 1837 and was restricted to male students only. It took just over five years more before the equivalent Female School was opened in Somerset House, and even then there were restrictions on the intake which confined candidature to indigent middle-class young women who came to learn a skill with which they would be able to earn their own living. Quite early in its history, the Female School, under its Superintendent Mrs Fanny McIan, started a wood-engraving class. It is probably significant that by 1848 the Art Union was urging that the class be abolished on the grounds that there were sufficient male engravers, and women were therefore not wanted. The Management Committee, however, supported its continuation on the grounds that wood-engraving was 'one of the means . . . by which we may give employment to women in this country'. It was a small beginning: in 1849 the class had nine pupils who spent three days each week learning to draw and two days on the practice of engraving. But what these young women were preparing themselves for was reproductive engraving. However sensitive their work, they would remain servants to a creative artist. In July 1852 this female class in wood-engraving, complete with its instructress, Miss Waterhouse, was transferred to Henry Cole's Central Training School. No woman can be singled out from these classes for exceptional artistry or engraving skills.

One female name to emerge from this period in the history of wood-engraving is Eliza Thompson and she was not a pupil at the Female School of Design, but daughter of the famous John Thompson. Thompson was not only one of the great reproductive engravers, but he also drew many of the illustrations which he supplied to publishers as engravings. His daughter was undoubtedly taught by him and probably helped her father on commissions in which he was illustrator as well as engraver. 'T.DEL.ET.SC.' is inscribed on many of the illustrations to William Yarrell's *History of British Birds*. 'T' might stand for any member of the family but in the Preface Yarrell's thanks are to 'Mr John Thompson and his sons, for the skill, the zeal, the success, and I may add the pleasure, with which they have laboured throughout this very long series of engravings'. It is as if, having become an engraver, Eliza had slipped on the guise of masculinity. On several of the pretty vignettes occurs the monogram which has always been understood to be for John Thompson but it could equally well be interpreted as ET. One can only speculate.

Vignette: The edible nest of the Chinese Swallow — signed with the Thompson monogram, from William Yarrell's *History of British Birds*, 1843.

Eliza's experience, being born into a family of wood-engravers, learning the craft thanks to that association, and becoming a respected but anonymous part of the family team, was one which many women may have experienced. It was to continue for the rest of the century. Georgiana Burne-Jones recalled the Morrises' first years in the Red House, Bexley Heath. 'Oh, how happy we were, Janey and I, busy in the morning with needlework or wood-engraving . . .' Despite the impressive number of studies which have been made of Morris and his circle, we have no idea what engravings these far from anonymous ladies were working on. They may have been black line compositions suitable for book illustration. Noel Rooke was later to point out that much of the Arts and Crafts movement's enthusiasm for reviving the art of wood-engraving sprang from a renewed awareness of the beauties of Renaissance illustrated books and woodcut prints. In the 1860s Morris was experimenting with engraved decoration, in a Renaissance black-line mode, for *The Earthly Paradise*, which he was then writing. Probably in 1864 or 1865 he and Burne-Jones had already designed decorations for a lavish, illustrated edition of this cycle of 24 stories, exchanged between Norse exiles and their Greek hosts. Georgiana Burne-Jones reported that, by the autumn of 1865 when the Morrises were preparing to leave the Red House, the plan was for it 'to be illustrated by two or three hundred woodcuts, many of them already designed and some even drawn on the block'. Perhaps Georgie and Janey had been practising engraving with a view to helping in the project. It does not seem to have been in women's nature at the period to reveal the extent to which they gave technical assistance to either fathers or husbands: the role of unpaid adjunct was simply accepted, especially when the involvement was a happy one. However, Sydney Cockerell recorded that one at least of the Cupid and Psyche blocks was engraved by Janey's sister Elizabeth Burden; and May Morris identified, by writing the information on the back of the block, that another was by Lucy Faulkner.

Cupid going away, illustration designed by Edward Burne-Jones and engraved by
Elizabeth Burden for the projected edition of *The Earthly Paradise c.* 1865.

The emergence of women as notable artist-engravers began in the last
quarter of the nineteenth century, and marches in step with the Arts and
Crafts movement, and with Women's franchise. But one has to admit that
for the simultaneous disappearance of the reproductive engraver there
were less glamorous causes. The craft, as a commercially viable trade
necessary to popular publishing, died. In the climate of the times at the
turn of this century the true liberator was photogravure whose commercial
application had been established in the 1880s. By 1901, when the Brothers
Dalziel published their *Record of Work 1840–1890* they had to admit 'the
days of wood-engraving are practically over . . . our occupation is gone'.
Through photogravure line blocks could be made of actual drawings,
while the more sophisticated collotype could reproduce anything captured
by the camera. To be a reproductive engraver had ceased to be a secure
profession. Coincidentally men ceased to worry about the infiltration of
women into the trade.

Psyche rushing out of Palace, illustration designed by Edward Burne-Jones and engraved by Lucy Faulkner for the projected edition of *The Earthly Paradise*, *c.* 1865.

Initially it was the Arts and Crafts movement, with the multitude of influences and interests which gave it life, that helped to fill any vacuum the demise of reproductive engraving might have left. In England the private press movement became so vigorous and widespread that it formed, at the end of the nineteenth century, a European focus for such interests. The artists, the climate, the technicians, the market and the materials were all to be found in London. The private presses, Vale, Eragny, Kelmscott and Ashendene were based on the homes of their founders, and each to some degree run as a family project in which women became involved as well as men. Morris had welcomed the work of women from his undergraduate days. When he launched the first number of the *Oxford and Cambridge Magazine* in 1856 it included decorated capital letters which had been engraved on wood by Mary Byfield, although at the time she was not given credit for the work. Simultaneously John Ruskin was beginning to promote the importance of the visual arts

THE OXFORD AND CAMBRIDGE
MAGAZINE.

SIR PHILIP SIDNEY.

PART II.—THE LEARNER.

CHAP. 3.—*Boyhood.*

R. MACAULAY, in his famous Third Chapter, gives us a picture, painted in his own bold and striking way, of the very country gentlemen, so self-willed and stupid, and that to their prejudices we owe it, that through those dangerous times the great heart of England beat ever steadily on, and

Decorative heading and capital letter engraved by Mary Byfield for the Chiswick Press, and used on opening page of No. III, *The Oxford and Cambridge Magazine*, March 1856, edited by William Morris. The heading was designed by Charlotte and Elizabeth Eleanor Whittingham.

for all members of society. Later, in 1869, when he was elected the first Slade Professor at Oxford, he showed no aversion to addressing women students as well as men. It was unusual in Oxford at that date; but Ruskin realised that a woman's mental capacity was not inferior to a man's. He had cheerfully lectured to girls' schools, and had written entire programmes based on his experiences: *Ethics of the Dust* published at Christmas 1865 had been a series of essays, inspired by conversations with school girls, about geology and crystallography. Ruskin, realising that society would only become aware of its responsibility for the visual world around, whether in terms of improving a rustic lane or vetoing a bad urban architectural design, if sensibilities were awakened to visual values, preached awareness and individual responsibility. Women were more sensitive to everyday problems than men, and could be equally, or more, vociferous in making a point. Ruskin appealed to women, sharpened their sensibilities, and programmed them for protest.

Meanwhile educational openings for women were expanding. What we now know as the Central School of Art was inspired by the Art Workers' Guild, an all-male association formed in 1884 by two architects, Morris's friend Philip Webb, and the younger, 27-year-old, William Lethaby. They had objected to the Royal Academy's refusal to exhibit crafts alongside arts, and now instituted the first school to offer, specifically, training in the crafts. Students were to receive training in the production methods for which they were designing. It opened in 1896 with Lethaby as its first Principal. Although wood-engraving was not to be taught there until 1912, Lethaby's early choice of staff and firm direction of studies was to have a profound influence on the development of the art. He selected promising young men with fresh ideas. The modest Edward Johnston was enticed to the Central in 1899 to teach calligraphy. Johnston, who had had no formal training, was almost amazed to find himself on the staff. His reward was a quite exceptional intake of students. His first class only

Lion Street, Rye by Mary Berridge, an early pupil of Noel Rooke.

· 16 ·

numbered seven but two of those were Noel Rooke and Eric Gill. Both found in Johnston's teaching a source of strength and inspiration that was specific and utterly simple: he taught that the shape of letters and style of calligraphy depended intimately on the form of the implement with which the scribe wrote. It was a bald statement of the interdependence of cause and effect – that the form of an art work must depend on the nature of the tool used to make it. The logic of it had a lasting influence upon the separate styles of engraving which Gill and Rooke were later to practise. Truth to the medium was to rescue wood-engraving from the slavish reproductive doldrums into which it had fallen in the course of the nineteenth century.

Rooke was unusually fortunate for an Englishman in having wider horizons: he had been educated in France, at the Lycée de Chartres as well as in London, and throughout his life read and discussed French works as well as English. He was able to use his knowledge of contemporary French developments to make valuable comparisons in his analysis of artistic development, and it must have been partly due to this that Lethaby gave him his first teaching appointment in 1905 at the early age of 24. His responsibility was to be book illustration. By this time the advantage of wood-engraving as a relief block which could be locked up with metal

Tail pieces by Vivien Gribble for *Sixe Idillia of Theocritus*, published by Duckworth & Co., 1922, printed at the Cloister Press, Heaton Mersey, Manchester.

The Wheatfield by Vivien Gribble, a highly stylized design reminiscent of late fifteenth-century Venetian illustrations.

type and printed in one operation seemed, at least in England, a thing of the past. Rooke had already, in 1904, become interested in engraving for its own sake, but it was not until 1912 that he was given permission to start a class at the Central. Collotype, which had been developed in the 1880s, was by this time so respected in England that even wood-engraved images were reproduced in books by that means. The reproductive qualities of the wood block being no longer of any seeming advantage, engraving could be looked at purely for its artistic possibilities. When in 1926 Noel Rooke's lecture to the Print Collectors' Club, *Woodcuts and Wood Engravings*, was printed in a limited edition of 500, the sixteen plates were all reproduced by collotype and either sewn in with, or tipped into, the text sheets. Rooke certainly did not look upon wood-engraving as any convenient short cut to book illustration.

Many of our leading engravers were taught by him, and if one lists some of his best-known pupils – Lady Mabel Annesley, John Farleigh, Robert Gibbings, Vivien Gribble, Dorothy Haigh, Muriel Blomfield Jackson, Lynton Lamb, Clare Leighton, George Mackley, Rachel Marshall, Margaret Pilkington and Guy Worsdell – one may conclude that the subject and the instructor attracted men and women equally. Both Rooke and the philosophy on which he based his teaching were influenced by the tenets of the

Cock and Hens by Margaret Pilkington. Well drawn, the rich contrast of black and white is heightened by the retention of a solid border around the image.

Tail piece by Margaret Pilkington who was to act from 1924–52 as Secretary, and 1952–67 as Chairman to the Society of Wood Engravers.

Houses in Hilly Country by Millicent Jackson. Framed like an easel painting, this is conceived more in terms of a drawing than a wood-engraving.

late nineteenth-century Arts and Crafts movement, and what he did at the Central School was an extension of that. His teaching was seminal, coming at a time when wood-engraving was ripe for revival not as a craft, but as an art. What Noel Rooke told the Print Collectors' Club on 20 January 1925 was his own mature analysis of the state of engraving. 'There is only one way of getting a thoroughly satisfactory engraving: the designer and engraver must be one and the same person.' His conclusion, summed up in the final paragraph of the lecture, affirms the quest for that unique quality in engraving which we will see has been the aim of the twentieth century. 'A good print,' said Rooke, 'is as unlike a drawing as anything can be. Good draughtsmanship is, if it were possible, even more necessary in making a print than in making a drawing . . . it is a combination of apparently contrasted qualities, aloofness and vitality, which makes a good print unlike anything else in the world.'

Very soon Rooke's earliest pupils in the wood-engraving class were receiving commissions from publishers and being acclaimed publicly. Perhaps because of the novelty of seeing women as artist-engravers they were given at least a fair share of the praise. In 1919 Geoffrey Holme, editor of *The Studio*, brought out a special number, *Modern Woodcuts and Lithographs by British and French Artists*. The selection and commentary is by

The Broken Mountain by Lady Mabel Annesley. This powerful expressionistic approach was allied to work on the Continent, particularly Germany in the late 20s and early 30s. The Second World war arrested the further development of this style in Britain.

Malcolm Salaman who praised Rooke as 'doing very valuable work as a trainer of young wood-engravers at the Central Technical School', and drew particular attention to four of his female pupils, Mary Berridge, Vivien Gribble, Margaret Pilkington, and Millicent Jackson. Robert Gibbings and Herbert Kerr Rooke were also praised and reproduced, but more important than any of these was another woman singled out by Malcolm Salaman, Gwendolen Raverat. Five years later Herbert Furst was to admit in the Preface to *The Modern Woodcut*:

> Mr Malcolm Salaman was good enough to bring Mrs Raverat's woodcuts under my notice; they excited in me an interest in xylography as a means of free aesthetic expression. Mr Salaman was thus the 'first cause' of the following study and to him as the indefatigable champion of print-makers I dedicate this book.

Lucky Mr Salaman! But Gwen Raverat could pride herself on the fact that she was the real inspiration for the book.

· 21 ·

Gwen Raverat had not been taught to engrave at an English art school. Reynolds Stone, writing just after she had died, reported that her wood-engraving was self taught and that she took it up having been at the Slade School for a year, studying painting under Frederick Brown and Henry Tonks. Herbert Furst, however, writing in 1923, far closer to the event, recounts that she began to engrave four years earlier than that, in 1905, and that she had been taught by Mrs E. M. Darwin, presumably Elinor Monsell, the wife of her eldest cousin, Bernard. The simple, amateur work

The Bath by Eleanor Monsell Darwin, who may have been the first to show Gwen Raverat how to engrave.

of E. M. Darwin was even illustrated by Furst as a significant precursor. What matters about Gwen Raverat's engraving, and what attracted Salaman and Furst so much, was the strength and originality of her painterly directness. She took her burin and used it to expres form impressionistically in terms of light. Malcolm Salaman selected *The Poacher*. 'The light speaks as her graver or gouge cuts away the wood, and her picture takes form and life.' This was not the approach Rooke was teaching his pupils. They were still using their engraving to describe the forms they were depicting. Gwen Raverat in *The Poacher* only engraves the moonlight as it falls on forms, consequently she creates a very powerful atmosphere in a tiny print which even Millicent Jackson, using a far larger area in her *Houses in Hilly Country*, fails to achieve. Instead of being decorative or hieratic symbols, as Vivien Gribble's were, Gwen Raverat's best prints convince one that they result from direct observation. Allied to this naturalism is a power to stimulate the imagination: the solitary figure of a girl in *Sheep* may be a shepherdess or a walker, but the low slant of the evening sun catches the trees and her body alike and gives both a monumentality which remains timeless. The little print is as fresh today as when Malcolm Salaman first reproduced it.

The praise which the critics afforded women engravers in this new school of printmakers must have been both exciting and encouraging. Even so, old attitudes died hard. Englishmen found it difficult to acknowledge women as innovators in the arts. Herbert Furst is typical. For all his unalloyed enthusiasm he wrote of Gwen Raverat:

> one of her first cuts, *The Knight of the Burning Pestel*, is a piece of wood chopping such as one would expect from a talented English boy . . . *The Cobbled Yard*, another early wood-cut, leaves no doubt as to the femininity of its author, but it has masculine independence of expression, and a clearly indicated will to obtain a perfect control over her medium. This control the artist has achieved, and it is this which makes her merit unusual as a woman's and outstanding as an artist's.

Gwen Raverat was evidently lucky to have been born a Darwin, eccentric, uninhibited, direct. As women artist-engravers had not emerged in the nineteenth century, no feminine style had been set: there was no pre-conception about women as wood-engravers. Women, having neither to conform to nor react against an established style, were free to explore and to inaugurate new modes. In 1911 Gwen Darwin married Jacques Raverat, and in 1915 they went to live in his native France. Herbert Furst, without remarking on any connection, reproduced the work of a French family, the Rouquets from Carcassonne. Looking at their work, and especially that of Jane, the daughter/sister of the trio, one immediately identifies Gwen Raverat's affinity with a French style. Back one goes to the impressionistic technique of depicting form in terms of the incidence of light. Indeed Gwen Raverat's most remarkable engraving in this mode was certainly made in France of a French scene, *Jeu de Boules, Vence, in Sunlight* (1925). Here nothing is outlined; not one figure remains static because each is revealed only by the sunlight which strikes it. The distant figures under the shadow of the trees are seen as dappled, indistinct, and their motion continuous.

The French prints, many of which were made after Herbert Furst's publication, capture the atmosphere of Vence where the Raverats lived for five years during Jacques' final illness. *Vence, The Town in Summer* (1924) although it is a block with more shadows than light, catches the intense brilliance and heat of noon-time summer in a small French town. Sadly, many of the blocks for these French scenes are in very bad condition. Several had to be printed from magnesium blocks in Reynolds Stone's 1959 selection of her wood-engravings, and an examination of the original

The Travellers by Gwen Raverat. This early print is bolder and more incisive than her later style and one may see in it that 'wood chopping' referred to by Herbert Furst.

The Poacher or *The Edge of the Wood* by Gwen Raverat, 1915.

Sheep by Gwen Raverat, 1919.

Jeu de Boules, Vence, in Sunlight by Gwen Raverat, 1925.

boxwood soon explains why: the wood has warped, split and distorted. Engraving blocks are often built up of small pieces, stuck, or better still, grooved and tongued, together. The block for *Vence, The Town in Summer* (1924), for instance, is made up of five separate pieces, one of which has itself split. Three small blocks, forming the lower part of the print, have shrunk, leaving the upper part ⅛ of an inch wider, and a split has naturally opened between the two halves. The block is unprintable, and the distortions irremediable. Blocks do not like travelling, and they hate changes of temperature. Boxwood has to be well seasoned before blocks are made up, otherwise disasters ensue. The tale of the demise of many of Gwen Raverat's French blocks may help to explain why wood-engraving has principally flourished in the cooler northern parts of Europe, and why most engravers cherish their blocks like delicate patients.

After her husband's death in 1925 Gwen Raverat and her two young daughters returned to England where she became the art critic of *Time and Tide*, and a prolific book illustrator. Kenneth Grahame had already selected a *Book of Poetry for Children* which had been published in 1916 by the Cambridge University Press. Gwen Raverat was commissioned to illustrate a new edition which appeared in 1932. Meanwhile she had been working

La Rigole du Lampy by Jane Rouquet. The shimmer of light with which this print is filled is as liquid as a scraper-board drawing. Gwen Raverat's decisive cutting in *Jeu de Boules, Vence, in Sunlight* is more direct and effective.

on blocks for the Ashendene Press's *Daphnis et Chloe*. Taking longer to print, it only appeared in 1933. After that she was busy with illustrations throughout the 1930s, occasionally finding time to produce a larger print of the Cambridge river scene which she had known since childhood. *The Fen* (1935) shows how powerfully she could use the linear patterning of stark winter willows, contrasted with the humped rotundity of sheep.

Vence, the Town in Summer by Gwen Raverat, 1924.

The Dead Ass by Gwen Raverat, 1937.

The Dead Ass by Gwen Raverat as printed in Lawrence Sterne's *A Sentimental Journey* published as a Penguin classic, 1938. All the whites have been rather coarsely strengthened, until it looks almost a different block. Although all the blocks in the printed edition are similarly worked over, it would appear that the strengthening of the whites was done by Gwen Raverat herself: *Le Désobligeant* in the Penguin edition is signed with the initials 'G.R.' A comparison of the two states of the print will show how difficult the reworking of a wood engraving can be. The book gives a poor account of Gwen Raverat's work.

Meanwhile wood-engraving classes progressed at English art schools and many women took advantage of the growing interest in woodblock prints which Gwen Raverat had helped to stimulate. In the late 20s and the 30s several publishers began to commission illustrations. Just as Gwen Raverat's direct and original approach to engraving had aroused critical interest in the genre, so now another woman's frank sensualism and articulate self-expression, in words as well as images, gave a strength and direction to engraving which it might well not otherwise have had. Many

Le Désobligeant by Gwen Raverat, 1937.

Le Désobligeant by Gwen Raverat, signed with initials, as printed in Lawrence Sterne's *A Sentimental Journey*, published as a Penguin Classic, 1938.

The Back of the Farm by Gwen Raverat, the original engraving made 1933–4 for A.G. Street's *Farmer's Glory*.

Harvest Supper by Gwen Raverat, the original engraving made 1933–4 for A.G. Street's *Farmer's Glory*.

Farm Building by Gwen Raverat, the original engraving made 1933–4 for A.G. Street's *Farmer's Glory* here shown as reprinted from the block in 1955 for a calendar for the following year.

Farm Building by Gwen Raverat, as printed in the 'New second reset edition mcmlvi' published by Faber & Faber. Almost all the whites have been recut, and the overall effect is of unnatural or artificial light. The edition, printed by Latimer Trend & Co. Ltd., Plymouth, was evidently not printed from the blocks but from strengthened electrotypes and, significantly perhaps, the title page bears the words 'With decorations by Gwendolen Raverat'. The engraver should be judged only on the basis of prints from her original blocks.

To Meadows by Gwen Raverat for *The Cambridge Book of Poetry for Children* edited by Kenneth Grahame and printed and published by the Cambridge University Press, 1932. Reynolds Stone recorded, 'When Walter Lewis was University Printer he liked using the wood surface to print from'. Certainly books printed in his day at the Cambridge University Press give faithful impressions of Gwen Raverat's work. Here her direct engraving on the block, spiking in light and texture with a spitz-sticker, can readily be seen.

Curly Locks by Gwen Raverat for *The Cambridge Book of Poetry for Children*, 1932. The charming imagin-ation and the engraver's ability to depict fantasy in the persuasively realistic terms of a design clearly expressed in line, are here demonstrated.

The Smuggler by Gwen Raverat for *The Cambridge Book of Poetry for Children*, 1932.

Ode on the whole duty of Parents by Gwen Raverat for Frances Cornford's *Mountains and Molehills*, printed and published by the Cambridge University Press, 1934.

Near an old prison by Gwen Raverat for Frances Cornford's *Mountains and Molehills* printed and published by the Cambridge University Press, 1934.

Mountain Path 'This is the hour when the children come
Each from the school to his especial home.'
by Gwen Raverat for Frances Cornford's *Mountains and Molehills*
printed and published by the Cambridge University Press, 1934.

The River Bridge by Gwen Raverat for 'Little Claus and Big Claus' in *Four Tales from Hans Andersen*, printed and published by the Cambridge University Press, 1935.

The Fen by Gwen Raverat, 1935.

writers, no doubt misled by the youthful vigour with which she has always conducted her life, credit Clare Leighton with slightly fewer years than she herself declares in *Who's Who*. She was born in the spring of 1899 to parents whose trade was words and whose lives were chaotic and uninhibited. Her father, Robert Leighton, wrote boys' adventure stories and combined this with journalism. At the time of Clare's birth he was literary editor of the *Daily Mail*. Her mother, in Clare's own account:

> wrote the melodramatic serials that appeared in the English newspapers owned by Lord Northcliffe . . . The entire household revolved around my mother's writing, for it was the large sums of money she earned that supported us. My father's work was not supposed to matter nearly as much, because he earned far less.

This situation inculcated in Clare a healthy streak of female independence, and she did not hesitate to practise it. She went to Brighton School of Art and then to the Slade but, perhaps through a music teacher of whom she had been particularly fond at school, Miss Elsie Rooke, she also met Noel Rooke who directed book illustration at the Central School. Clare Leighton joined those to whom he taught wood-engraving. What she brought to the work was a very powerful dynamism. She seems to have designed and engraved with her whole being and, in her writings too, the enormous physicality of her response to visual and emotional experiences comes over so strongly that she must have taught many women how to unleash a hitherto unacknowledged power within themselves: 'freed for the moment from my own work, I can identify myself with everything about me, and become all that I see,' she wrote. It does not sound very revolutionary; but, for a middle-class woman of her generation, her perception of experience was sensational. Take the description of a hill walk in France on a spring evening in her semi-autobiographical memoir *Sometime–Never*.

Decorations by Annabel Kidston for Matthew Arnold's *The Forsaken Merman* and *The Scholar Gipsy*, published by John Lane as vol. IV of the 'Helicon Series' in 1927. The small engravings owe much to the work of Edward Gordon Craig.

The Sea grows stormy, the little ones moan by Annabel Kidston for Matthew Arnold's *The Forsaken Merman* 1927. She uses her tools cleverly to produce a variety of textures – fine lines to express the moving liquid waves, chipping into the wood to suggest the rough torso of the merman, and the point of a tool spun in the wood to create the circular scales of his tail.

Higher and still higher we climb. We have left beneath us the terraced fields and the vines, the peach trees and the blossomed almonds. The path grows less clear; we lose it and then find it, to be faced once more with thorn bush and tangle of maquis. Hot from our climb, we throw off our coats. So long as the sun can warm it, we will let the thorn bushes scratch our skin. He is bare to the waist, and his sunburnt body is the colour of the small pockets of earth that nestle between the rocks. It is as though he were that earth, walking. Spring on a mountain side in Provence, and the earth around us bursts to bud and blossom, sweating with fecundity. It is as though one hardly dares to tread on this earth, lest one should stamp down some sprouting seed, some swelling bulb, some quickening root. And the earth seems to be drawn up into our bodies, till we, I and this man beside me, sweat with the same fecundity. Up to the barren plateau on the mountain top I will carry my body, this earth, and out from the sheltered valleys

A Traveller by Annabel Kidston, 1930.

Headpiece by Elizabeth Rivers, for 'The Picnic' a short story by Walter de la Mare published in a limited edition by Faber & Faber, 1930.

Headpiece by Elizabeth Rivers for 'An Ideal Craftsman' a short story by Walter de la Mare, published in a limited edition by Faber & Faber, 1930. Elizabeth Rivers had previously been commissioned by John Lane to illustrate *The Second and Seventh Idylls of Theocritus* which appeared as the first volume of their 'Helicon Series' in 1927.

Decorations by Helen Kapp for *The Scandals and Credulities of John Aubrey*, 1931. Direct engraving of a strongly expressionistic nature.

Crossing to Cardiff by Helen Binyon for Maria Edgworth's *Angelina*, 1932. The clashing diagonals splendidly suggest the instability of the boat.

Kenwood Folly by Enid Marx, 1930. With vigorous direct engraving Enid Marx produced rich textural compositions. Her powerful sense of pattern lent itself first to hand-blocked textiles and eventually led her to industrial design.

Cynthia by Lettice Sandford for *Thalamos* published by the Boar's Head Press, 1932. Lettice Sandford had studied at Chelsea Art School, where she learned to engrave. She and her husband Christopher, bibliophiles, admired the work of Eric Gill, and it is to him and to Blair Hughes Stanton that one has to turn to find comparable fine live white-line engraving. The printers at the Chiswick Press had difficulty maintaining the clarity of the white lines.

Leander by Lettice Sandford for *Hero and Leander* published by the Golden Cockerel Press, 1933.

The Road to Sorrento by Alison McKenzie, 1935. The strong flat patterning can be compared with the work of Robert Gibbings or Edward Wadsworth.

House over the Canal, Bath by Winifred McKenzie, 1948.

between my limbs, the rounded hills of my thighs and belly, will sprout bud and blossom and fruit. I carry my earth to the barren rocks of the mountain top.

By 1939 when this was published Clare Leighton was well respected as an artist on both sides of the Atlantic and Victor Gollancz must have felt that only the prurient could detect any element of impropriety in such writing. The passion from which it springs invests much of her engraved work.

In the late 20s she had already received several prestigious commissions for book illustrations from Heinemann, Longman, Macmillan, and Harper and Brothers of New York. These included Thornton Wilder's *The Bridge of San Luis Rey*, and Thomas Hardy's *The Return of the Native*. In 1930 Longman published in both England and America a folio volume *Woodcuts, Examples of the Work of Clare Leighton*, and she became the first woman to have a collection of her prints issued in such a way. A special introduction was provided by the celebrated author, Hilaire Belloc. The prints, pulled individually from the blocks, are on flimsy paper, each tipped into the volume with the titles printed on a fly sheet. The edition is limited to 450 copies, numbered and signed by the artist. It is an exceptional production in honour of a woman artist. Clare Leighton's upbringing must have had much to do with her early success. She knew from the start how to deal with the publishing world. Moreover she had travelled widely and her subjects often had an exotic fascination, providing glimpses of Toulon, or Genoa, Dalmatia, New York or Boston. Unlike Gwen Raverat she conceived her subjects mainly in line, and in strongly contrasted areas of black and white. Many of the prints are single works, neither conceived for, nor suitable for, book illustration. Single prints of this kind were evidently in vogue between the wars, and she herself was to explain their success:

> Yet another reason for the general interest in wood engraving lies in the modern fashion of interior decoration. The strong simple lines and proportions of the new architecture, with the more general use of positive plain colours are well suited by the equally strong blacks and whites of wood engraving. The increased use of white walls is in harmony with the dead black of the printing ink – a denser black than can ever be produced in an etching.

Although her early prints tend too much towards this 'denser black', Clare Leighton has never lacked enterprise: she knew how to attack a block as directly as Gwen Raverat. Look, for instance, at the little print of wind-swept sea and sky in H. M. Tomlinson's *The Sea and the Jungle* published by Duckworth in 1930. The actual composition may have been planned, but the drawing is done freely by the burin. This impression is on the soft pulpy paper of popular publishing, whereas the seven full-page plates in the same volume are on smooth, whiter paper, tipped in. On this smooth paper, finer white lines and textures could be relied on to print cleanly so long as the blocks were not over-inked. In the small, vigorously-cut block, however, Clare Leighton was producing something specially adapted for printing on the soft pulp paper. Book illustrators soon learned to adjust to the production methods offered by publishers, and serious illustrators struck up a relationship with those houses who took a real interest in seeing that their original blocks were most faithfully reproduced. In the early 30s, when Victor Gollancz emerged as the chief commercial publisher promoting wood-engraved illustrations of great subtlety and delicacy, Clare Leighton became one of his authors; but before that happened she herself wrote a book for The Studio Publications which was to be influential in carrying appreciation of wood-engraving a step further. *Wood-engraving and Woodcuts,* first published in 1932, was the second volume of the 'How to do it' series and it heralds the total liberation of wood-engraving from the professionals. Not only was it now to be available to art students, but also to amateurs. The series aimed to make the practice of various art forms accessible to every man and every woman.

It is an attractive volume with a striking, block-printed cover showing engraving tool, sand bag and block in an overall repeat pattern. Contemporary photographs of the 'wood engraver at work', tipped in, show a handsome Miss Leighton in embroidered smock, intent upon her work. This introductory section is followed by a selection of prints,

> chosen . . . rather as illustrations of varieties of technique than for their interest as works of art. Careful study of these prints through a magnifying glass will give more help than any amount of reading.

It is a very remarkable achievement. She was the first woman to write about wood-engraving; and this was a new kind of book. From then on people could actually 'teach themselves': the process of wood-engraving is described for the ordinary reader in a simple and straightforward fashion and the result is a clarity lacking even in Chatto and Jackson's *A Treatise on Wood-Engraving* of 1839. What makes the advent of her book even more remarkable is that it is the first twentieth-century technical guide which adds a running commentary, in the form of captions, upon actual contemporary prints. She provided an index to the serious aims and achievements of living engravers.

The following year, 1933, Collins published *The Farmer's Year,* an oblong folio containing the twelve most ambitious book illustrations she was ever to produce. They are powerful and subtle at the same time, and are beautifully printed, fortunately, for her admiration of intense blacks persists here, and had the finely engraved white lines not shown up,

February: Lopping by Clare Leighton for *The Farmer's Year, a Calendar of English Husbandry* published by Collins, 1933.

March: Threshing by Clare Leighton for *The Farmer's Year, a Calendar of English Husbandry* published by Collins, 1933.

Horsechestnut Flowers by Clare Leighton for *The Farmer's Year, a Calendar of English Husbandry* published by Collins, 1933.

Japanese Anemone by Clare Leighton for *Four Hedges* published by Victor Gollancz, 1935.

Oriental Poppies by Clare Leighton for *Four Hedges* published by Victor Gollancz, 1935.

gloom rather than monumentality would certainly have resulted. The text, written by Clare Leighton herself, is secondary, although complementary, to the plates. Through the descriptions of the agricultural labours during the twelve months of the year runs a thread of village life, and archetypal characters emerge: Daisy, an old cow, is cosseted in freezing January and finally in a damp December another Daisy is sent to market for slaughter and a farmer's wife weeps. There is great nobility about the prints and descriptions, but the cumulative impression is bleak. Take *February: Lopping*. The print is brilliant in composition (the rounded hills and pointed hay stacks in counter-rhythm to the rough leaning willows and their curving branches) and brilliant in contrast (the cold white glare of the snow against the rich black of the gnarled trees). The total effect is harsh, and the text drives home the point:

> Giant willows border the mill stream. The piles of willow hurdles for the sheepfolds are wearing low. So the farmer lops. The grim, individual shapes of the willow trees lean in a row over the black unfrozen waters of the running stream, seared and wrinkled, like a family of mourners. One by one the upspringing branches within reach from the ladder are slashed off. The lopper next stands on the platform of the tree-top, like an elongation of the dark tree itself, and chops at the few remaining branches until the last one towers alone and grotesque, like the single tooth in an old man's sunken mouth. This collapses, too, and the tree stands compact.

In England after the Depression Clare Leighton had poured out her sympathy for the stark, grinding poverty of agricultural labourers; she had done for farming what Käthe Kollwitz had done for women and children in poverty-stricken Prussia.

The Farmer's Year, like her Studio volume, is a new concept in a book illustrated for adults. It resembles a magic lantern show: the pictures are the most memorable thing, but they are animated, made more memorable by the words which accompany them. It may even have been a slide lecture which suggested the form of *Wood-Engraving and Woodcuts*. Whatever the inspiration, Clare Leighton brought fresh ideas to an old art, and her vigorous approach was appreciated. In 1936 Studio Publications produced a special winter number, *Wood Engraving of the 1930s*, written by her. It expands on some of the themes broached in her 1932 book. Printing from wood blocks, she asserts, is very much to the taste of the times: 'with its severity of discipline it appeals to the modern artist, whose interest is primarily in strong organised shapes'. It is no surprise to see her drawn towards Expressionism: 'To be alive and crude' she wrote, 'is better than to be dead and refined.'

This is not to say that Clare Leighton discounted fine engraving, merely that she flung the door open wide to admit not only the delicate work of

Mussel Gatherers, Toulon by Clare Leighton, 1926.

Sunday before the fair it rained by Clare Leighton for Robert Nathan's *The Fiddler in Barley* published by Heinemann, 1927. Misleadingly described on the title page as '6 drawings', the illustrations in this volume are all wood-engravings. This one later appeared in Longman's 1930 *Woodcuts of Clare Leighton*.

Hampstead Heath by Clare Leighton, 1930, produced as a travel advertisement for the London General Omnibus Company.

Stormy Sea by Clare Leighton for H.M. Tomlinson's *The Sea and the Jungle* published by Duckworth, 1930. The volume was printed in offset by Phototype Limited of Barnet, Herts.

Vegetable Marrows by Clare Leighton for *Four Hedges* published by Victor Gollancz, 1935.

Sloe by Clare Leighton for *Four Hedges* published by Victor Gollancz, 1935.

A Lapful of Windfalls by Clare Leighton for *Four Hedges* published by Victor Gollancz, 1935. Sub-titled 'a gardener's chronicle', this overtly autobiographical calendar shows Clare Leighton at her happiest. The written account, acutely observant, is hopeful and enthusiastic, while the engravings themselves, admirably printed by the Camelot Press, have become lighter and brighter, the former tendency towards funereal black being counterbalanced by the removal of background, allowing scene or plant to shine out against the white of the paper. The book became an instant success running to four impressions followed by a 'cheap edition' between October 1935 and autumn 1936. All the editions are beautifully printed and, apart from details of editions, appear to be identical.

Chair Bodgers by Clare Leighton for *Country Matters* published by Victor Gollancz, 1937. Naturally the success of *Four Hedges* led to a sequel which, although never publically as successful, was equally beautifully produced.

Turning the Plough by Clare Leighton for *Country Matters* published by Victor Gollancz, 1937.

A Bunch of Primroses by Clare Leighton for *Country Matters* published by Victor Gollancz, 1937.

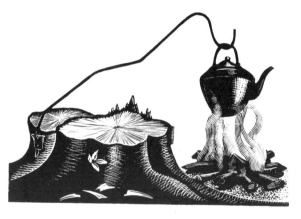

Kettle on Wood Fire by Clare Leighton for *Country Matters* published by Victor Gollancz, 1937.

Decorations by Clare Leighton for Thomas Hardy's *Under the Greenwood Tree*
published by Macmillan, 1940; printed by R. & R. Clark, Edinburgh. The beauty
of Clare Leighton's black upon white engravings again responds to fine printing,
before war-time economy standards were imposed.

Illustrations by Clare Leighton for Gilbert White's *The Natural History of Selborne* published by Penguin Books in March 1941; printed by R. & R. Clark, Edinburgh. The difference in quality of printing brought about by war-time restrictions is perfectly demonstrated by a comparison of these engravings with those in *Under the Greenwood Tree*. The same printing house handled both.

Agnes Miller Parker, but also Expressionism. Upon one of Agnes Miller Parker's prints she comments, 'This is about the cleanest work that is being done today, and at the same time the most solid. It combines sensitiveness with precision and is conscious throughout of realised form.' Agnes Miller Parker, four years older than Clare Leighton, was a very different character and had a very different career. She was to become one of the most respected of British engravers, but had little voice in any contemporary development. She was born in Ayrshire in 1895 and went to the Glasgow School of Art when she was 19. At the end of her four-year course she married a fellow student, William McCance and for the next twelve years taught first at the Glasgow School of Art, and then as art mistress in two English schools. Her first published prints are cut in linoleum for Rhoda Power's *How it happened*, published by Cambridge University Press in 1930. The designs are simple, vigorous and balance well on the page. It speaks much for her industry and real love of wood-engraving that she was never again tempted to make a series of illustrations in lino. That year, 1930, she and her husband were employed at the Gregynog Press in Newtown, Montgomeryshire. There they were to stay until 1933 and she was able to concentrate more on engraving, illustrating two Gregynog books, *The Fables of Esope* and *Twenty-one Welsh Gypsy Folk Tales*.

At the same time she worked on outside commissions. Robert Gibbings admired her work; and, as he owned the Golden Cockerel Press at that period, he commissioned her to illustrate Rhys Davies' *Daisy Matthews* and H. E. Bates' *The House with the Apricot*. This last, though she only made four engravings for it, led to greater things. Victor Gollancz commissioned her to illustrate H. E. Bates' *Through the Woods* and *Down the River*. For *Through the Woods* she produced 73 of her finest engravings and for *Down the River*, 83. Both books are perfectly printed and extraordinarily beautiful. Unlike Clare Leighton she does not show man at work so much as nature in its vulnerable delicacy. There is an intensity of vision, heightened by a very controlled degree of stylisation and a sure sense of drawing and design which prevents her work from sliding into mere prettiness. The illustrations lead one further into the world about which her author wrote. Perhaps more than anything she loved cats, and she seems to have shared in their silent, solitary and inscrutable nature. It comes as no surprise that her recreation was fly fishing: only with infinite stillness, silence and patience could she have observed the wild life of Britain as she depicted it. Hedgerow and river bank were a whole world for her and she seldom looked beyond. The illustrations she produced for several Hardy novels are impressive but generally fail to take one any nearer, conceptually, to the text. One of her happiest associations during the Second World War was with Herbert Furst, the very man who in the early 20s had written so perceptively on *The Modern Woodcut*. Now, in 1944, Frederick Muller

Cock Pheasant

Passage of tiny Feet

Chapter headings and decorations by Agnes Miller Parker for H.E. Bates' *Through the Woods*, 1936. The gradation of texture and shading in these engravings is as remarkable for clarity of definition as for subtlety.

Kingcup, Kingfingers, and Kingfisher

Cuckoo

Cock Sparrows

published a collection of his 'essays on various every-day subjects, mostly connected with the countryside'. It was probably Furst himself who suggested that Agnes Miller Parker should be commissioned to provide 'decorations'. The result was 47 tiny but beautiful blocks, responding with quick intelligence to the essays themselves and cut a degree more boldly than those velvety illustrations for the H. E. Bates books. No doubt she realised that wartime printing methods were cruder and more hasty, and that on poor quality paper subtleties would be lost. It makes an immediate impact in every way, this little volume of essays, and must have cheered many people when it appeared.

Agnes Miller Parker's obvious ability to cope with wartime restrictions of book production imposed by the 'authorised economy standards', brought her immediately after the war an important series of commissions, five volumes of the country essays of Richard Jefferies, published by the Lutterworth Press between 1946 and 1948. Many of the blocks are larger, even up to full-page size; and they make the volumes, for their period, an exceptionally fine series of commercially published books. Other artists fared far worse. Gollancz, for example, published Clare Leighton's *Southern Harvest* in 1943 before full economy standards were imposed, but the results are poor. Perhaps the best pressmen had been called up. Leighton's love of large areas of black proved disastrous in wartime circumstances; blocks are over-inked, the impressions are uneven, pages are slurred and type badly locked up. The illustrations look smudged rather than sharp. That this was a fault, not inherent in the block, but only in a combination of the block with wartime printing, can be seen by comparing *Cotton Pickers* (1941) issued as a presentation print for the *20th Anniversary of the Print Club of Rochester* in 1951. Obviously an engraving made at the same time as those in *Southern Harvest*, it is here carefully inked, crisp in definition and expressive of the relentless sunshine rather than a slur upon the artist.

Clare Leighton's life and work has probably been affected by war at least as much as any other woman engraver's. In her most impressionable teenage years she had experienced the First World War and seen its real trauma brought home in the death of her charismatic and gifted elder brother, Roland. We should be aware that for such a highly sensitive personality, this would have intensified the shadows in her world even if the two women closest to him, his mother first, and then his fiancée Vera Brittain, had not both written of his life. His mother's fictionalized account, begun only two or three weeks after his death, was finished in three months, and then was followed by her nervous collapse. Vera Brittain's much more considered and moving account, *Testament of Youth*, came out in 1933.

It is no surprise that Clare Leighton has seldom succeeded in ridding herself of dark shadows, or that with them she should, in the middle of the

Ollie by Clare Leighton for *Southern Harvest* published by Victor Gollancz, 1943, printed by Richard Clay and Company Ltd.

Cotton Pickers by Clare Leighton, 1941.

Alabama Hog Pen by Clare Leighton for *Southern Harvest*, 1943.

The Coocooburrah (linocut) by Agnes Miller Parker for Rhoda Power's
How it Happened printed and published by the Cambridge University
Press, 1930. Clarity of both vision and decision is shown in these prints,
whether in the brilliant fling of the cresting wave, or the waddle of
hippos. In each print one can see that her technique was that of an
engraver, rather than a cutter with the knife point.

Hippos (linocut) by Agnes Miller Parker for Rhoda Power's *How it
Happened* printed and published by the Cambridge University Press,
1930.

Wave (linocut) by Agnes Miller Parker for Rhoda Power's *How it Happened* printed and published by the Cambridge University Press, 1930.

The Fiery Dragon by Agnes Miller Parker for *Welsh Gypsy Folk Tales* published by the Gregynog Press, 1933.

Fox by Agnes Miller Parker for H.E. Bates' *Through the Woods* published by Victor Gollancz, 1936; printed by the Camelot Press. Both the H.E. Bates volumes illustrated by Agnes Miller Parker are treated in style and size as companion volumes to Clare Leighton's *Four Hedges* and *Country Matters*. The publisher employed the same printers for all four volumes.

Fox Cubs by Agnes Miller Parker for H.E. Bates' *Through the Woods* published by Victor Gollancz, 1936.

Tree Fruits by Agnes Miller Parker for H.E. Bates' *Through the Woods* published by Victor Gollancz, 1936.

Title Page by Agnes Miller Parker for H.E. Bates' *Down the River* published by Victor Gollancz, 1937.

White Water-Lilies and Dragonfly by Agnes Miller Parker for *Down the River*, 1937.

Harbour by Agnes Miller Parker for *Down the River*, 1937.

Sea Gulls Flying by Agnes Miller Parker for *Down the River*, 1937.

Low Tide

Rats on Rafters

The Bridge, Henley-on-Thames

Trout

Rowing Boat

Flying Heron

Decorations by Agnes Miller Parker for *Down the River*, 1937

Cows in Stream

Decorations by Agnes Miller Parker for Herbert Furst's
Essays in Russet published by Frederick Muller Ltd.,
1944, printed by the Camelot Press.

· 71 ·

Second World War, express the grinding poverty among cotton picking negroes:

> cotton pickers . . . are dragged to earth by the heavy pick-sacks, unable to soar . . . I know that I watch a world of symbols, and the great sacks that hold these people to the earth bind them in many ways. I know that I watch struggle made manifest . . . I see that man over there, bent to the earth, and it is as though the curves and shapes before me are eloquent as no words or thought can be. The curve runs from head and back, into the half filled sack that ties him to earth.

Her art, with its emotive exaggeration, could not adjust to wartime conditions. Instead she was drawn in wartime to subjects which chimed with her most sombre tones. She illustrated with drawings Marie Campbell's *Folks do get born*, published by Rinehart & Company in 1946. It is an account of the lives, poverty and nobility of elderly negro midwives in Georgia. The rich darks in her work are there even when the medium is not wood-engraving. Not surprisingly the blocks for the 1941 Penguin edition of *The Natural History of Selborne* by Gilbert White look too heavy for the page both in size and in density. That she was unaware of these defects is confirmed by her reproducing one of them, *Mice*, in the 1944 edition of *Wood-engraving and Woodcuts*, as an example 'of how suitable the woodblock is for decorating the printed book . . . it will print clearly and well on quite ordinary paper, and stands up to a large run of printing'. In general, with respect to engraved blocks, the statement is true. Many artists did modify their work during the war, making it more suitable for reproduction in economy standard books. That Agnes Miller Parker was particularly successful at this was probably thanks to her work at the Gregynog Press, a side of book production which Clare Leighton had never had opportunity to experience. Certainly the 1939–45 war saw a great revival of wood-engraving for book illustration, and it is probably no exaggeration to say that two World Wars in the span of a single generation had a profound influence not only on the style, but also the content of engravers' work.

Clare Leighton's friendship with Vera Brittain continued because both were in sympathy with the same ideals: pacifism, feminism, racial and sexual equality, natural justice in all its aspects. Others were similarly involved. Gertrude Hermes moved rapidly from *naif* but vigorous depictions of plants, to symbolic depictions of spiritual states of being. Her friend Naomi Mitchison, whose published works have included *Comments on Birth Control* (1930) and *The Moral Basis of Politics* (1938), trod the same path as Vera Brittain. Their concerns were those broached in the late nineteenth century by such groups as the Fabians, but seen from a feminist viewpoint. Like so many women who were in their teens and

The Slough of Despond by Gertrude Hermes, 1928.

Waterlilies by Gertrude Hermes, 1930 – REDUCED to 90%.

One Person by Gertrude Hermes, 1937 — REDUCED: diameter 35 cms.

Stonehenge by Gertrude Hermes, 1963 – REDUCED: 35.3 × 25.5 cms.

Honour thy Father and thy Mother by Dorothea Braby 1956, adapted from her print
of the same subject for *The Commandments* published by F. Lewis, 1946.

twenties when they experienced the First World War, both were motivated and liberated by those times. In 1936 Gertrude Hermes illustrated Naomi Mitchison's *The Fourth Pig*, 'this little pig had none': it was the period when several women engravers became involved in political and social aims, and sincerely attempted to express their beliefs. If they wished to be serious artists, without denying their own natures, women had to transform attitudes and expectations. 'The reorganisation of society in such a fashion that its best women could be both mothers and professional workers,' wrote Vera Brittain in 1933, 'seemed to be one of the most acute problems which my generation – and to a lesser but still important extent all subsequent generations – had now to face.' Both Gertrude Hermes and Blair Hughes-Stanton, whom she married in 1926, had been pupils of Leon Underwood at the Brook Green School. Underwood, by the early 20s, had already evolved a personal, symbolic style, and Blair Hughes-Stanton moved on from this to develop a particularly English version of Surrealism. Gertrude Hermes, who mastered the craft of engraving better, and became a greater artist than either man, endeavoured to project through her engravings an expressionistic sensation of individual experience and concern. *One Person* of 1937 is an enormous print (14 inches in diameter) which represents not simply a swimmer, but the solitary struggle, through a wealth of conflicting forces, to keep integrity and forward progress simultaneously. The strength and originality of her approach can clearly be seen if compared with Agnes Miller Parker's 1938 illustrations to Gray's *Elegy*. It is a remarkable series symbolizing the poet's thoughts in a country churchyard, but every aspect of the prints has a dream-like quality, the engraving is smooth, controlled, and regular, giving a general impression of sad solemnity, emotion recollected in tranquillity, very different from the visual shock of Gertrude Hermes' conflicting textures built up from vigorous jabs, stabs and strokes of the burin, and heightened by rich areas of untouched black.

Not only Gertrude Hermes but also Dorothea Braby expressed in their work the dual responsibility of men and women for their children, for the future. *Honour thy Father and thy Mother* was engraved by Dorothea Braby as late as 1956, but developed a theme she had been pursuing since 1937 when she first began to work as an illustrator for the Golden Cockerel Press, then owned by Christopher Sandford. She was a wonderfully warm and enthusiastic idealist who in 1960 gave up professional art to devote herself to social work. In the 1950s, however, she was most active, writing and teaching the history and practice of wood-engraving. Again The Studio was the publisher, issuing in 1953 a substantial, profusely illustrated, quarto volume, *The Way of Wood Engraving*. This included a large number of the symbolic and expressionistic prints made since Clare Leighton's 1936 survey of the 30s. Dorothea Braby had great kindness and energy, as

I know from personal experience, in replying to inquiries from young students. I expect she directed many more than myself to the wonderful workshop of the last surviving traditional British block-making firm, T. N. Lawrence & Son in Bleeding Heart Yard off Greville Street. Hers was an introduction which opened a door whose hinges could on occasion prove stiff. Within dwelt, from 7.30 am to 5.30 pm each weekday, a craftsman who did more to keep wood-engraving alive than any individual writer or engraver in the last hundred years, Stanley Lawrence.

Although he was extremely shy, Stanley Lawrence's enthusiasm for and knowledge of wood-engraving and wood-engravers – untinged, apparently, by any ulterior hopes of inordinate commercial gain – made him the household god and the fount of wisdom of every wood-engraver whom he befriended. Luckily for women he seemed particularly susceptible, in an avuncular and innocent fashion, to supposed female charm – a propensity confirmed by his grandson Simon Lawrence who wrote in *Matrix 7*, 'He fostered many engravers both young and old (but especially young and female).' The magic thing about Stanley Lawrence was that, in his eyes, one remained young for years and years, itself an enormous psychological boost! But on blocks and prints his standards were consistently high, and he never hesitated to criticize poor work or a falling-off of quality. His blocks varied with the nature of the wood, but one could always rely on their being beautifully seasoned, matched and meticulously made. Many promising young students must have found their early trials eased by the rare treat – sometimes a gift – of a block exceptionally fine in grain and consistent in texture. Perhaps it is not too fanciful to attribute the large number of contemporary women engravers in part at least to their encouragement by the late Stanley Lawrence.

High in the pantheon of Stanley Lawrence's most prized and admired customers stood Joan Hassall. Producing the very finest of engravings for a wide variety of applications, she became the best-loved British engraver of her generation. Her training was the most archaic still available in 1931. At the age of 21 she had gone first as a probationer (1927) and then as a full student (1928) to the Royal Academy Schools, where she remained for five years. Wood-engraving, still a 'craft', was not taught there; and it was almost by chance that she learnt the technique. A fellow student persuaded her to go to an evening class at the School of Photo-Engraving in Bolt Court, off Fleet Street. The instructor, Ralph John Beedham, has been described by her as 'a commercial engraver who spent his working years doing reproductive engravings largely for catalogues'. She also declared, 'We had first-rate technical instruction and nothing at all about the subject as "art".' Beedham had, however, been taught letter design and letter cutting by Eric Gill at Ditchling, and was to remain his assistant in that for the rest of Gill's life. He also, at the urging of the Ditchling

Stanley Lawrence at Bleeding Heart Yard by Anne Jope, 1977. One of those engravers 'young and female' whom Stanley Lawrence delighted in encouraging, Anne Jope has woven a medly of evocative images, her tribute both to boxwood and to the block-maker.

community, wrote *Wood Engraving* with an introduction and appendix by Eric Gill which Hilary Pepler's Press published in 1921. The book proved a success and ran to several reprints with Faber & Faber as its publisher. Under such meticulous and experienced instruction, Joan Hassall flourished. When he showed his class a capital letter he had himself engraved, 'a feeling of absolute certainty more like remembering, came to me that I too could engrave like that'. From that time on wood-engraving was her principal *métier*. In her last year at the Royal Academy Schools she saw the work of Thomas Bewick, first enormously enlarged in a slide, part of a lecture by Francis Dodd, and then in Selwyn Image's 1924 edition of *Memoir of Thomas Bewick*. Having bought this she 'was astonished to find pages of reproductions at the end, thus initiating one of the great admirations and pleasures of my life'. She does not tell us whether she realized that the blocks in Image's edition are themselves enlarged, most in the proportion 7 to 5; but these blown-up versions were probably less daunting for a young student 'inhibited by the cost of wood' than the breath-taking delicacy of the originals might have been. She studied Bewick in the light of two invaluable remarks often repeated by Francis Dodd, first 'catch the monumental moment', and second, Orpen's belief that 'the light is the most important character in a picture'. Having begun with Bewick, she continued to study the engravings not of her contemporaries but of the great nineteenth-century engravers and the pleasing archaism of her work recommended her particularly as illustrator, for some of our greatest classic women novelists. Her first commissioned engraving was a title page for a book of poems by her brother, Christopher. It came out in 1936 and the consequences were exceptional in the history of English wood-engraving: Heinemann, the publishers, asked Francis Brett Young to write *Portrait of a Village* specifically as a vehicle for Joan Hassall's engravings. Working on beautiful large blocks supplied by T. N. Lawrence & Son she made ten illustrations and, on small integral pieces of box, seven vignettes. Unlike Bewick, she did not lower any part of the blocks to achieve lighter inking and consequently, although fine, her engravings always remain sharp. Since they call for great clarity of press work and evenly calibrated paper, Joan Hassall's engravings, despite their archaisms, were made only for the techniques of her own time.

This does not mean to say that her work during the war took no cognizance of economy standards. *Cranford*, published in 1940, was largely engraved before wartime restrictions had begun to bite. But after her move to Edinburgh in 1940, where she taught printing and engraving at the College of Art throughout the war years, she produced simpler, less textured and atmospheric engravings, which owe more to the chap-book than to the greater subtleties of Bewick. That this was a deliberate decision based on a knowledge of craftsmanship available can be seen by a comparison with work commissioned in the post-war years: Mary Russell Mitford's *Our Village*, originally published in the first quarter of the nineteenth century, was issued by Harraps in 1947. In it she returns to all the delicacy of engraving and nuance of drawing found in the Brett Young volume of ten years earlier.

Alas, her expectations of the renaissance of printing outran what the presses were capable of delivering. Disappointed in what even the long-experienced R. and R. Clark of Edinburgh were able to achieve for Harraps under the 'authorised economy standards', she refused to illustrate *The Vicar of Wakefield*, a commission offered by the same publisher. Her own standards were always fastidiously high and her intolerance of poor work made her a hard task-master for students and printers alike. Nor did she scruple to apply the most severe self criticism, even when arthritis threatened to prevent her from engraving. She had been brought up in a household familiar with every commercial method. Her father, John Hassall, was a celebrated poster artist and popular illustrator. He must often have made drawings on scraper-board, that medium so much used at the turn of the century – card primed with fine-ground plaster of Paris which is then smoothed to a high glaze with a cool iron and drawn upon with brush and india ink. The advantage is that the black ink, when dry, may be scratched into to make white detailing, very much as a burin cuts the light into a boxwood block. While her hands were bad during the early

The Night Drive by Joan Hassall for *Portrait of a Village*, 1937. Sensitivity to atmosphere is seen here in Joan Hassall's view of the silent night-bound village seen in the headlamps and across the bonnet of the Doctor's car.

The Stricken Oak by Joan Hassall for Francis Brett Young's *Portrait of a Village* published by Heinemann Ltd., 1937, printed at the Windmill Press.

The Water Splash by Joan Hassall for *Portrait of a Village*, 1937.

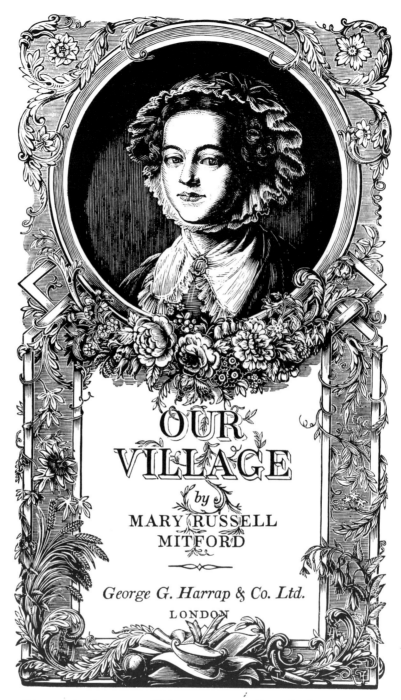

Title page by Joan Hassall for Mary Russell Mitford's *Our Village* published by Harrap & Co. Ltd., 1947, printed by R. & R. Clark, Ltd., Edinburgh

The road winding downhill by Joan Hassall for *Our Village*, 1947.

A cottage – no – a miniature house, all angles by Joan Hassall for *Our Village*, 1947.

A tuft of primroses springing . . . from the mossy roots of an old willow by Joan Hassall for *Our Village*, 1947.

Down we sat, on the brink of the stream, under a spreading hawthorn by Joan Hassall for *Our Village*, 1947.

I am sure that this is the wood sorrel by Joan Hassall for *Our Village*, 1947.

'What can have become of my keys?' by Joan Hassall for *Our Village*, 1947.

Tail piece to 'Old Master Green' by Joan Hassall for *Our Village*, 1947.

The shop! – all prosperous, tranquil, and thriving by Joan Hassall for *Our Village*, 1947.

Quebec House, Westerham, Kent scraper-board drawing by Joan Hassall for *Sixteen Portraits* edited by L.A.G. Strong, published for the National Trust by The Naldrett Press, printed by Richard Clay and Company, Bungay, Suffolk, 1951.

Small Moments

Crab-apple Blossom

Burning the Bines

Measureless Caverns

Wind and Water

An Encounter in Venice

Headings by Joan Hassell for Richard Church's *Small Moments* published by Hutchinson, 1957, printed by William Brendon & Sons Ltd. Joan Hassall's imaginative verve, as well as her skill as an engraver is evident in the heading to *Wind and Water* where the total drenching effect of the rain is indicated by its diagonal drive overrunning the oval of the headpiece. Equally in *Burning the Bines* smoke drifts up beyond the limits of the regular headpiece.

50s she made amazing illustrations in this manner, rendering the drawings entirely in terms of wood-engravings: it had become her natural mode. Many admirers never realize that the architectural plates in *Sixteen Portraits,* edited by L. A. G. Strong and published for the National Trust by The Naldrett press in 1951, are scraper-board drawings. The advantage was that the 'engraved' scraper-board image could be 'repaired' by a sweep of india ink in a way that no boxwood block ever could. Equally, her additional illustrations, made to harmonize with the old blocks already selected for *The Oxford Nursery Rhyme Book* of 1955 are miraculously devised on scraper-board. Even although the resulting images could only be printed by a reproductive process, they show, more clearly than anything else could, that Joan Hassall thought in terms of engraving.

However, the most sensitive of her work was always done on boxwood. Happily the problems with her arthritic hands were overcome in the late 50s, and she managed to engrave for another twenty years. As though, in the years of physical restriction, she had been longing for those subtleties beyond the scope of scraper-board, she celebrated her restoration with a breathtaking suite of wood-engravings: Richard Church's *Small Moments,* published by Hutchinson in 1957. The book of essays must have struck a sympathetic chord; it certainly stimulated Joan Hassall's visual imagination and produced, very many times, that 'monumental moment' which made her feel as elated as the mystic, Dame Julien of Norwich when, gazing at a walnut shell cupped in the palm of her hand, she had a vision of the entire world. Such intensity is particularly womanly, and well represented in Joan Hassall.

There was a generation whose normal educational progress was interrupted because of war. Monica Poole, fifteen years Joan Hassall's junior, was working in a factory which made parts for fighter aircraft during the years when she would otherwise have been a young art school student. After the war, in her mid-twenties, she moved resolutely in the direction her more mature chief interests lay, choosing to study engraving under John Farleigh in the Book Production course at the Central School of Arts and Crafts. Very soon she established her personal preference not for monumental moments but for statements of timelessness in nature. The fascination seen by Ruskin in a geological specimen was intensified by Henry Moore when he turned an interesting flint about and about in his hand and, from that suggestion, projected immensely magnified forms which dwarf the individual spectator. Such intense concentration upon a natural object until, to the exclusion of all else, it fills the mind, does not belong solely to mysticism. It was appreciated not only by Henry Moore, Barbara Hepworth and Jim Ede, but by a whole generation who longed to escape from functionalism. Of the engravers Monica Poole best exemplifies the mood. Many find her trance-like view of her subjects – rocks, shells, deserted sea shores, twisted trees, desiccated leaves or the suffocating sweetness, anemone-like, of magnolia flowers – sinister. This surprises her. But it is certain that her engravings never merely depict a scene or object: George Mackley, knowing her well and sensitive to the subtleties of engraving, asserted that in her prints she 'has moved far from the purely perceptual into the strongly conceptual'. A piece of chalkstone on her desk becomes *Piddock Architecture* and after an illness she returned to engraving with *Dry September*. The one carries all the burden of the millenia of pre-history. The other suggests not only the pain, impermanence and contortion, but also the majesty, of dying plant life. Distilled from her personal post-operative depression, it is so highly conceptualized as to have become symbolic. Into such symbols the viewer may read his or her own experience, for the personal nature of the artist's inspiration has been sublimated. Like Gertrude Hermes', Monica Poole's engravings are mostly large, single prints, independent of literature and innocent of patronage: she works from herself, for herself. She is deservedly the most sought-after of contemporary wood-engravers.

The scene today is not only lively and various, but widespread. In the United States, wood-engraving, though not an art in which one could find instruction or appreciation nationwide, was taught for many years by Leonard Baskin at Smith College in Northampton, Massachusetts. Smith, one of the oldest American colleges, has always been, and still remains, exclusively for women. It is not an art school but an academic institution of high prestige. Even so, Baskin has launched a few pupils. Gillian Tyler engraves. She also runs her own small Cricket Press in Thetford, Vermont. Her work tends towards fantasy, a leaning she has had since a student at Smith in the mid-50s: her graduation work at the end of Baskin's course was an illustrated edition of Edgar Allan Poe's *Hopfrog*. In the 60s she engraved eight beasts from the Old Testament and issued them as *A Bible Bestiary*, followed in 1971 by fifteen animals engraved for T. J. Elliott's *A Medieval Bestiary* printed and published by David Godine in Boston. Her works are beautiful: controlled as engraving, but often interesting as much for their rich, wild net of lines and finely contrasted textures, as for their obvious pictorial inventiveness. The more Germanic, expressionist side of Baskin's influence can be detected in another, more recent pupil, Mary Azarian. Her favourite medium is the woodcut but, although she works on the plank, much of the technique depends on engraving or embossing rather than exclusively on cutting.

On the West Coast a very different engraver, Sarah Chamberlain, runs another private press, mainly to print and publish her own work, pouring new wine into old bottles. The engravings have that precise, neat quality so fascinating to many small children. Sometimes there are charming colour prints, engraved in linoleum as well as boxwood. Her texts are

Magnolia by Monica Poole, 1972.

Dead Trees, Sheppey by Monica Poole, 1977.

Dry September by Monica Poole, 1980.

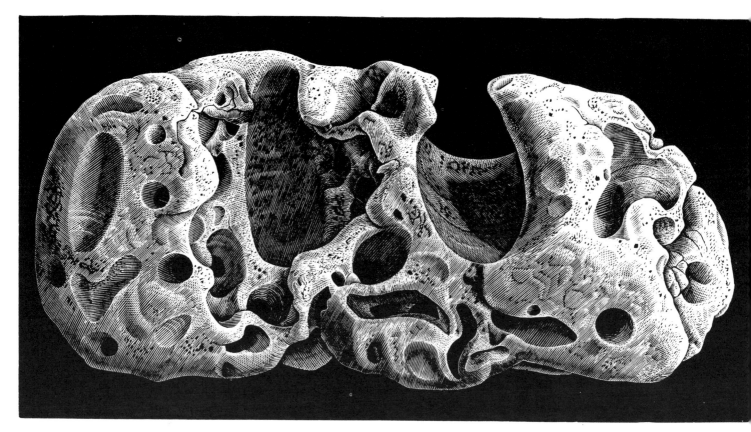

Piddock Architecture by Monica Poole, 1975.

Dry Leaves by Monica Poole, 1980.

Chalk Coast by Monica Poole, 1983 for George Mackley's *Monica Poole wood engraver* printed and published by the Florin Press, 1984.

Serpens by Gillian Tyler for T.J. Elliott, *A Medieval Bestiary* printed and published by David Godine, Boston, 1971.

Columba by Gillian Tyler for *A Medieval Bestiary*, 1971.

traditional tales such as *Stone Soup* or *The Three Bears*, their novelty lying not only in the freshness of engraved illustrations, but in the retelling of the stories themselves: rather than having a marred little Goldilocks as invader, the three bears are burgled by a mean old crone. The story is transformed from a cautionary tale to improve the headstrong child, to a laughable incident about three dear bears. At the same time the adult reader is challenged to a thoughtful reappraisal of moral values, and may begin to question which section in modern society is represented by the beasts. The engravings, similarly, appeal to the adult as much as to the child, although differently. The minutiae of the engravings command admiration and close study, which slows the adult down to a child's pace, and carves out time for thoughtful pondering.

A ram caught in a thicket . . . by Gillian Tyler for *a Bible Bestiary with eight beasts from the Old Testament* printed and published by the Cricket Press, Thetford, Vermont, 1962.

Cetegrandia by Gillian Tyler for *A Medieval Bestiary*, 1971.

Sirena by Gillian Tyler for *A Medieval Bestiary*, 1971.

I . . . *Icicles* by Mary Azarian for *A Farmer's Alphabet* printed and published by David Godine, Boston, Massachusetts, 1981 — REDUCED to 70%.

U . . . Underwear by Mary Azarian for *A Farmer's Alphabet*, 1981 — REDUCED to 70%.

The Three Bears by Sarah Chamberlain for *The Three Bears* printed and published by The Chamberlain Press, Portland, Oregon, 1983.

The Old Woman looking in by Sarah Chamberlain for *The Three Bears*, 1983.

Down she came, plump upon the ground by Sarah Chamberlain for *The Three Bears*, 1983.

The Soldiers of Fortune by Sarah Chamberlain for *Stone Soup* retold by Kenneth Jones, printed and published at The Chamberlain Press, Portland, Oregon, 1985.

Making the Stone Soup by Sarah Chamberlain for *Stone Soup*, 1985.

In the southern hemisphere, Australia has recently produced three remarkable women print-makers who work in wood, or a wood substitute. As box is foreign to them, they have all experimented with different substances. Edwina Ellis originally trained as a jeweller, came to England to study metal-engraving at the John Cass College, London, and then flitted to wood-engraving at a Marlborough Summer School where she worked with Anne Brunskill and Simon Brett. Requiring large blocks, she found box expensive, or could not find box at all. So, used to manipulating a variety of materials, she experimented with commercial products, and has recently espoused Delrin, an extruded plastic developed for industrial use. Conceiving her images with a fascinating amalgam of surrealism and neo-classicism, or else an academic clarity, she has been making colour prints since 1983, building them from three primary colours alone.

Meanwhile, at Lock's Press, Brisbane, powerful prints in illustration of archetypal rhymes or simple stories told by Samuel Johnson or Leo Tolstoy are cut in marine plywood by Margaret Lock. Her husband, an Englishman, is the printer, and the binding or boxing of the books is so idiosyncratic as to heighten the physical impact of the work. An uninhibited physicality with regard to prints is also displayed by Rosalind Atkins who was taught by Tate Adams at the Royal Melbourne Institute of Technology. She launched into her print-making career with some large traditional engravings in black and white; but recently she has begun to experiment with embossed prints from engraved blocks. They have a positively sculptural effect, being deeply impressed into thick pulpy paper. Such things can only be achieved by using industrial materials. At the chattering stage of some party one of her admirers told me that she has tried the effect of print-making by reversing a tractor over an engraved block on a soft surface. It was sincere adulation: an Australian legend is in the making.

In Britain progress has been hampered, since the death of Stanley Lawrence in February 1987, by a shortage of professional-quality boxwood blocks. Many well-established engravers devoutly hope that supplies will materialize again. Experimentation is tolerable when necessity drives, but for most engravers there is no adequate substitute for box. It would be impossible to imagine so fine and subtle an artist as Claire Dalby, for instance, engraving on anything else. Like Bewick, she is a water-colourist who plans her compositions in such detail that she is able to control recession and shading in her final prints by lowering certain areas of a block so that neither inking nor impression should be heavy. Her tones are often a beguiling silver, and the quality of her work, with its variety of beautifully modulated textures, cannot be equalled by any woman engraving today. She is not an illustrator, but makes small single prints which repay close study, by carrying one's imagination on happy expeditions through her favourite haunts. She is a slow, methodical worker, but

FEIGNED SIMPLICITY: "*Feigned Simplicity is a Delicate Deception*" by Edwina Ellis
from *The Maxims of the Duc de la Rochefoucauld*, 1986.

Two Clementines, engraved on Delrin® (Trademark: acetal manufactured by DuPont) by Edwina Ellis, 1988.

One Clementine, engraved on Delrin® (Trademark: acetal manufactured by DuPont) by Edwina Ellis, 1988.

Charity by Edwina Ellis for *Garden Prigs* 1986–87.

of such clarity and artistry that nothing pedestrian shows in the exquisitely finished prints.

Other engravers working on less complex subjects, designing in less depth, and working with far greater speed, lend themselves to the commercial world. In the 1960s I used to receive an enchanting house-news letter, incorporating wine catalogue and seasonal recipe sheet. It came from Christopher & Co Ltd. of Jermyn Street, and was particularly delightful when decorated, as so often it was, by one of Yvonne Skargon's wood engravings. She has a style which in a past age might have been in great demand for decorations upon precious metals: it is fundamentally linear, flat and shallow. In wood-engraving, such a style adds the rich contrast of black and white to its range, and the results are often decorative motifs of the greatest charm. A high degree of precision is called for in the work, for it is a style which allows of no mistakes. Another such perfectionist is Sarah van Niekerk. She studied at the Central School under Gertrude Hermes who was a marvellous teacher, inspirer and technician. Many of Gertrude Hermes' fine qualities are kept alive by Sarah van Niekerk, who herself taught wood-engraving at the Royal Academy Schools from 1976

Pantry by Rosalind Atkins, 1986.

Little Tommy Tittlemouse (woodcut) by Margaret Lock for *Fame's Trumpet* printed and published by Locks' Press, Brisbane, 1982.

Hector Protector (woodcut) by Margaret Lock for Fame's Trumpet, 1982.

Two of my most liberal benefactors silently advancing with a net behind me (woodcut on marine plywood) by Margaret Lock for Samuel Johnson's *The Fountains, a fairytale* printed and published by Locks' Press, Brisbane, 1984.

She felt herself continually decaying (woodcut on marine plywood) by Margaret Lock for *The Fountains*, 1984.

We peasants have no time to let any nonsense settle in our heads (woodcut on marine plywood) by Margaret Lock for Leo Tolstoy's *How much Land does a Man need?* printed and published by Locks' Press, Brisbane, 1986.

He was ten times better off than he had been (woodcut on marine plywood) by Margaret Lock for *How much Land does a Man need?*, 1986.

Pahom and the Bashkir Chief (woodcut on marine plywood) by Margaret Lock for *How much Land does a Man need?*, 1986.

The Old Chair by Claire Dalby, 1971.

Borgund Stave Church by Claire Dalby, 1971.

Old Boat Sør Flatanger by Claire Dalby.

The Gazebo, West Dean, by Claire Dalby.

Durham Cathedral by Claire Dalby, 1983. Areas of the river and the trees immediately below the Cathedral have been lowered on the block before engraving, giving a fine silver tone when printed.

November by Yvonne Skargon for Christopher & Co. Ltd.,
Wine & Food, 1966.

August by Yvonne Skargon for Christopher & Co., Ltd.
Wine & Food, 1967.

Rose and Butterfly by Yvonne Skargon, for cover of
'Hortus' magazine, No. 6, 1988.

to 1986. Her compositions, whether illustrations or uncommissioned prints, create a complete view of the subject in hand, while holding the totality together in firm unity. She is adept at handling different tools to produce a wide variety of very appealing textures, and she boldly changes modes of depiction even within one composition: in her illustration *Gaston de Blondeville* for the Folio Society's 1986 *The Complete Mrs Radcliffe*, the predicament of the falling knight is realistically suggested, the close-up details of texture carefully picked out, while his fainting lady in the spectators' stand is depicted in comic cartoon style, capturing the elements of crude histrionics.

Sarah van Niekerk's comedy is constrained by the text she illustrates. Other women working today take a frank delight in the funny side of real life. Among their predecessors was Eric Ravilious' wife, Tirzah Garwood. Her *At the Dog Show* of 1929 is a wordless smile at the large rather masculine lady powdering her diminutive terrier to sneezing perfection. Gwenda Morgan, her exact contemporary, learnt to engrave at the Grosvenor School of Modern Art under Iain Macnab, and her prints, too, bubble with quaint delight and good humour, rendered in very direct engraving of highly stylized compositions. Laughter is never far from another younger engraver, Miriam Macgregor. Encouraged and advised by Stanley Lawrence, she taught herself to engrave in the late 1960s. She works at the Whittington Press and has illustrated several enchanting publications: *Song of the Scythe* in 1983 is a lively short text by Bruce Mawdesley animated by six engravings. Countrymen wait apprehensively for 'the enemy'; the control of textures – plants, tree, sheep, and distant landscape – is lovely, and the humorous glimpse expands on the text:

> During many a civil war, when the cry had gone round for the peasants to take up arms, farm tools were the only weapons at hand, and along with the bill-hook and pitchfork many a scythe was carried into the fray, although I can't help feeling that many a friend as well as foe must have been struck down.

Two years later *Allotments* appeared. For me it is the most cheering little book of engravings to have been published this decade. Brassicas in all states of perfection and decay are drawn beautifully by Miriam Macgregor, and her sympathy for the denizens of the allotments is evident in the attention and care she gives to depicting their earnest work, their ingeniously constructed garden sheds, their triumphs and despairs. It is difficult to know what not to reproduce from among such cheering delights.

Fortunately, engraving is alive and well today, and we can look forward to other lively books from wood-engravers. One woman engraver in particular has been instrumental in nurturing this healthy state, Hilary

Jacobs in Shropshire by Sarah van Niekerk, 1979.

Gaston de Blondeville by Sarah van Niekerk for *The Complete Mrs. Radcliffe*
published by the Folio Society, 1986.

At the Dog Show by Tirzah Garwood, 1929.

Armed in a Civil War by Miriam Macgregor for Bruce Mawdesley's
Song of the Scythe printed and published by the Whittington Press,
1983.

Autumn Afternoon by Miriam Macgregor for R.P. Leister's *Allotments*
printed and published by the Whittingham Press, 1985.

Down at the Allotment by Miriam Macgregor for *Allotments*, 1985.

Sunday by Miriam Macgregor for *Allotments*, 1985.

Illustrations by Miriam Macgregor for *Allotments*, 1985.

Bright Interval by Gwenda Morgan, 1962.

Willingly to School by Gwenda Morgan, 1969.

Christmas Presents by Hilary Paynter, 1982.

Stress by Hilary Paynter, 1983.

Buck's Mills by Hilary Paynter, 1986.

Paynter. The Society of Wood Engravers, founded in 1920, and embracing relief print-makers of all sorts, was guided and guarded from 1924 to 1967 by Margaret Pilkington. After that it rather faded from sight until it was reformed in 1984, with Hilary Paynter as its Secretary. Engraving is a solitary, very intense pursuit, and engravers too easily become lonely and isolated, so a Society with lively exhibitions and some effective method of information exchange is an enormous asset. Instead of having to become reconciled to the life of a saintly mystic (walnut and all), or a stoical St Simon Stylites, the engraver can trade experiences and prints at meetings, or find a vehicle for requests and offers in the Society's newsletter, *Multiples*. In all this the efficient, cheerful work of the Secretary is essential. Perhaps such a Society always needs an energetic woman as its intelligent linchpin. Professionally, Hilary Paynter is both engraver and educational psychologist. Her interests cover a very wide range of subjects from the craggy landscape, *Buck's Mills* to a terrifying image of aberrant rats, *Stress*, 1983, or a wry political satire by way of a Christmas greeting. Her work, in all its aspects, deserves the greatest respect. Her energy gives others the chance to thrive.

It is impossible to leave the subject of women engravers without a thought for all those hundreds of women in both nineteenth and twentieth centuries who have learned the craft and remained unknown. Many may have achieved very little. There are, however, considerable artists still to be discovered. Especially in the first half of this century there were women who engraved magnificently, but not from necessity. Women from professional middle-class families went to art school for art's sake. Probably in the belief that to work for a publisher would be demeaning, they sought no public beyond their own immediate circle. From the time that he moved the firm to Bleeding Heart Yard in 1953 Stanley Lawrence remedied much of this, showing prints by promising unknowns to as many people as he could. But there were some customers who purchased blocks and tools only by post and never thought of giving him a sight of the finished prints. One such, Helen R. Lock, is known only as a watercolourist who exhibited at the Royal Academy, the Royal Watercolour Society, and the Royal Institute of Watercolours. She was a pupil and friend of Alfred Rich, and studied at the Westminster School of Art where Rich taught. As a wood-engraver she came to Stanley Lawrence's notice only several years after 1967 when she had died at the age of 83. Blocks, some engraved, some unused, were offered to him for sale. Typically generous, he bought them, and then let me have several of those that were engraved, requesting that I should try to publicize her talents as widely as possible, and attempt to establish her reputation posthumously. Helen Lock may stand for a regiment of unknown women engravers: by her works shall she be known.

Hellebore by Helen Lock (1884–1967).

Ruined Keep by Helen Lock.

Chow in winter by Helen Lock.

SELECT BIBLIOGRAPHY

ANON   *Elegant Arts for Ladies* [London, Ward & Lock, N.D. – but from advertisements bound at end, 1856]

BALSTON, Thomas   *A History of English Wood Engraving 1900–50* Image no. 5 [London, Art and Technics Ltd., 1950]

BEEDHAM, R.J.   *Wood Engraving* with introduction and appendix by Eric Gill [Ditchling, Ditchling Press, 1921]

BELL, Quentin   *The Schools of Design* [London, Routledge & Kegan Paul, 1963]

BEWICK, Thomas   *A Memoir written by himself*, edited, with an introduction by Iain Bain [Oxford University Press, 1975]

BRABY, Dorothea   *The Way of Wood Engraving* [London, Studio Publications, 1953]

BRETT, Simon   *Engravers, a handbook for the nineties* [Cambridge, Silent Books, 1987]

BRITTAIN, Vera   *Testament of Youth* first published by Victor Gollancz in 1933 [London, Virago Press, 1978]

BURNE-JONES, Georgiana   *Memorials of Edward Burne-Jones* 2 vols. [London, Macmillan & Co., Ltd. 1904]

CALLEN, Anthea   *Women in the Arts and Crafts Movement 1870–1914* [London, Astragal Books, 1980]

CARTER, Sebastian   *The book becomes. The making of a fine edition* [Cambridge, The Rampant Lions Press, 1984]

CAVE, Roderick   *The Private Press* [London, Faber & Faber, 1971]

CHAMBERS, David   *Joan Hassall, Engravings & Drawings* [Pinner, Private Libraries Association, 1985]

CHATTO, W.A. and JACKSON, John   *A Treatise on Wood Engraving, historical and practical* [London, Chatto & Windus, 1861]

DALZIEL, George and Edward   *The Brothers Dalziel, a record of work 1840–1890* first published London, Methuen and Co., 1901. Reprint with Forward by Graham Reynolds [London, B.T. Batsford Ltd., 1976]

FRANKLIN, Colin   *Printing and the Mind of Morris* [Cambridge, The Rampant Lions Press, 1986]

FURST, Herbert   *The Modern Woodcut* [London, John Lane at the Bodley Herd, 1924]

GARRETT, Albert   *A History of British Wood Engraving* [Tunbridge Wells, Midas Books, 1978]

LEIGHTON, Clare   *Sometime . . . Never* [London, Victor Gollancz, 1939]

LEIGHTON, Clare   *Tempestuous Petticoat, the story of an invincible Edwardian* [London, Victor Gollancz, 1948]

LEIGHTON, Clare   *Wood-Engraving and Woodcuts* [London & New York, Studio Publications, 1932]

LEIGHTON, Clare   *Wood Engraving of the 1930s* reviewed by Clare Leighton [London, Studio Publications, special winter number, 1936]

MACDONALD, J. Ramsay (editor) *Women in the Printing Trades: a Sociological Study* [London, P.S. King & Son, 1904]

MACKLEY, George *'Shall we join the Ladies?'* wood engravings by women artists of the twentieth century [Oxford, Studio One Gallery, 1979]

MCLEAN, Ruari *The Wood Engravings of Joan Hassall* [Oxford University Press, 1960]

PAPILLON, J.M. *Traité historique et pratique de la Gravure en Bois,* 2 vols. [Paris, Pierre Guillaume Simon, 1766]

RANDLE, John *The wood-engravings of Gwenda Morgan* [Andoversford, The Whittington Press, 1985]

ROGERS, Samuel *The Pleasures of Memory* [London, Cadell & Davies, 1810]

ROOKE, Noel *Woodcuts and Wood Engravings* Being a Lecture delivered to the Print Collectors' Club on January 20th, 1925 on the origin and character of the present school of engraving and cutting. [London, Print Collectors Club Publication No. 5, 1926]

SALAMAN, Malcolm *Modern Woodcuts and Lithographs by British and French Artists* Special Number of *'The Studio'*, edited by Geoffrey Holme [London, Studio Publications, 1919]

SALAMAN, Malcolm *The Woodcut of To-day at home and abroad* [London, Studio Publications, 1927]

STONE, Reynolds *The Wood Engravings of Gwen Raverat* [Cambridge, Silent Books, 1989]

WALLAS, Graham *The Great Society: a psychological analysis* [London, Macmillan & Co. Ltd., 1925]

WARREN, Arthur *The Charles Whittinghams* [New York, The Grolier Club, 1896]

For kindly permitting the reproduction of engravings in this book the author wishes to thank the individual artists and the following: Clover Hill Editions, Mrs Sophie Gurney, Mrs Patricia Kapp, Brian North Lee, Mr David Leighton, Mr G McClelland, Winifred McKenzie, Mrs Ursula Mommens, Mrs A Quickenden, The Rampant Lions Press, Mrs Judith Russell, Whitworth Art Gallery, Univ. of Manchester, Penelope Woolfitt.

Thanks are also due for help and advice during work on this book to: Simon Brett, Betty Clark, Derek Gibbons, Daniel Jaffé, Adrian Layton, The Society of Wood Engravers, Geraldine Waddington.